The Portsdown & Horndean Light Railway

The Portsdown & Horndean Light Railway

THEN AND NOW

ROBERT HIND

WITH BARRY COX

HALSGROVE

First published in Great Britain in 2020

British Library Cataloguing-in-Publication Data
A CIP record for this title is available from the British Library

ISBN 978 0 85704 335 1

HALSGROVE
Halsgrove House,
Ryelands Business Park,
Bagley Road, Wellington, Somerset TA21 9PZ
Tel: 01823 653777   Fax: 01823 216796
email: sales@halsgrove.com

Part of the Halsgrove group of companies
Information on all Halsgrove titles is available at: www.halsgrove.com

Printed and bound in India by Parksons Graphics Pvt Ltd

Introduction

One of the reasons for building the Portsdown & Horndean Light Railway (P&HLR) was to provide a direct fast link with the railway station at Cosham as no railway served the people at Hambledon, Denmead and Waterlooville. At the turn of the last century these villages were way out in the sticks as we say and to get to a railway station, either Havant or Cosham was a days journey on its own.

The light railway – essentially a tramway – that ran from Cosham to Horndean was only in existence for 32-years, and, although a success in its early days with the coming of more comfortable buses the company began to lose money and the service came to an abrupt halt in early 1935.

From 1924 some trams did run as a through service initially to the town (the Guildhall) and from 1925 to Southsea. In January 1903 the Portsmouth Corporation agreed to let their cars on the route to Cosham run up the hill to 'Point A' at Portsdown Hill Plateau. In May that year Corporation cars ran from Clarence Pier to 'Point A'. At this point, passengers wishing to travel onward had to change cars. Just south of the underpass bridge was a sign directing passengers to 'Change here for Green Cars.' The service was not all that popular and it was reported that in the third week of November, 1903 a total of 636 Corporation tramcars ran up and down Portsdown Hill without a single passenger. It must be remembered, however, that at that time the area was sparsely populated.

I begin this book with an abridged version of how The Portsmouth Street Tramway Company services began in the 1870s reaching Cosham station level crossing on 31 July, 1881.

There was a proposal to extend the line along Cosham High Street and Magdala Road along Park Lane to Havant Road. Powers were then sought to lay an extension on a private right-of-way up Portsdown Hill to the George Inn on the summit. It was to thence run by street tramway to Waterlooville. In July 1896 an hourly summertime horse bus service was started from Cosham to Waterlooville.

A new company entitled the Hampshire Light Railway (Electric) Company Limited had been incorporated on 17 May, 1897. Both this and the Portsmouth Street Tramways Company were wholly-owned subsidiaries of the Provincial Tramways Company Limited.

At an enquiry held at Cosham an approval was given for the construction of a 6-mile, 2.9 chains line to be laid between Cosham and Horndean. At first, it was hoped to run the line along Cosham High Street but because of the narrowness of the highway land was purchased to the west of the village. The line was to be on a private right-of-way.

Much of the ground the tracks were to be laid on was owned by Mr Thistlewayte of Southwick Estate who owned 8000 acres and he did not want trams running across his land. The War Office had clearance rights over the land and so any objections were over-ruled.

A terminus at Horndean was also objected to as it would have been adjacent to a chapel but as there was to be no Sunday working these objections were also over-ruled and construction of the light railway was assented to by the Board of Trade on 2 September,1899.

Even then, an argument over the gauge to be used meant that the line was not begun until January 1902 by

Dick Kerr & Co., Ltd to a gauge of 4ft 7¾ inches, one quarter inch narrower than the standard railway gauge. The reason for the unusual gauge was in anticipation of running railway wagons over the line. The wagons would run on the wheel flanges in the grooved rails. The gauge had been adopted in Portsmouth by the Corporation for the same reason.

Description of The Route

The Portsdown & Horndean Light Railway started life by leaving the Corporation tracks In Portsmouth Road opposite where the the Portsbridge Hotel (sometime spelt Ports Bridge Hotel) stands and opposite the junction with Highbury Grove. If you look at photographs of the junction it looks as if the line headed west for a hundred yards and then turned northward through what is now a park and sports ground. It ran just to the east of the line of poplar trees. This is more of an optical illusion as the Portsmouth Road has a curve and in fact it is just a V with the light railway tracks running parallel with the Corporation tracks.

An iron bridge was constructed to cross the L.S.W.R. railway line which at that time was four tracks wide with a head shunt either side of the up and down main lines. An embankment was constructed leading to the bridge. On the embankment an interchange platform was located known as 'Point C' with a sign stating 'Change Here For Green Cars.' Initially there were three tracks at this point and Corporation passengers were asked to change here if they were travelling further than Widley Lane. (On reflection, it seems strange to have passengers change at 'Point C' as the Corporation cars ran to 'Point A' at Widley Lane.)

On the north side of the railway line, Southampton Road (now Waite Street) was crossed with gates to protect the road. This location today would be in front of the Cosham Fire Station. (Spur Road and Northern Road were not then in existence. London Road came down into Cosham where it met the the Havant Road coming in from the left. London Road then continued down Cosham High Street to the level crossing where it became Portsmouth Road. When these two roads were constructed in 1922 they were made into level crossings.) After Waite Street the line then began its climb up Portsdown Hill until the Southwick Hill Road was reached.

This was also bridged and to the north of it a footbridge was put in place. After crossing the road the line continued up the hill on the left side of the London Road on the embankment where there was another bridge over a brick arch which crossed a public footpath which led to the site of the fairground. This underpass was later filled in. A flight of stone steps now marks the location of this bridge. Continuing on for another 200 yards 'Point A' was reached opposite Widley Lane. When 'Point A' was first put into place two former horse-drawn cars were used as shelters for waiting passengers. A flight of concrete steps which led up from London Road to this point remains intact to this day. After this point the track became single line with a passing loop half way between 'Point A' and the summit. The line continued on until about 200 yards from the George Inn at what is now a false summit.

Up until 1813, the road along the top of the hill was level with the summit at some 420-feet above sea level. Such trouble was given to stagecoach horses trying to reach the summit before the drop down to Widley, that Napoleonic prisoners of war were engaged in lowering the summit at this point by about fifty feet making it a little easier for the horses. The George Inn was of course built much later. In 1968, the George was by-passed by a new road to the east at an even lower level and the vista given to motorists of Portsea Island as they came over the hill was lost for ever.

When the line left the reserved track it became a double track street tramway for a hundred yards before becoming single again just before crossing Portsdown Hill Road. The line then went onward to Waterlooville in the middle of London Road with three passing loops before

Purbrook village was encountered. Between Purbrook and Waterlooville there were three other passing loops and then through Waterlooville village it became double track becoming single line again where Hulbert Road joins the London Road. At this point today there is a large roundabout controlling traffic. The former main road through the village has become a precinct and a new road runs to the west of it.

After Hulbert Road the line ran on a reserved single track on the right hand side (east side) nearly all the way to, but just short of, Horndean village. Just south of Park Lane, Cowplain a three-lane depot was constructed on the west side of London Road. This is now the site of a Lidl supermarket and nothing remains of the original building. The line never reached the centre of Horndean village but terminated just short of the Methodist Chapel which remains to this day. Plans for the line to continue through Horndean and onward to Petersfield never came to fruition.

Acknowledgements

All of the historic images, either postcards or photographs, in this book can be seen in many publications. Apart from one or two mentioned they have all been purchased by Barry Cox at public or on line auctions and are part of his vast collection. Every effort has been made to identify copyright holders. Should any have been accidentally overlooked, the omission will be corrected in future editions. Please contact me through the publisher.

All the modern photographs have been taken by myself, Bob Hind. I must thank Martin Petch for allowing me the use of a couple of photographs from his book *Gosport and Horndean Tramways* (Middleton Press) although Barry Cox has since purchased the same photographs or postcards. I have also relied on The *Tramways of Portsmouth* by S.E. Harrison for much valuable information.

I am grateful to the following:

Map of Route – J.C. Gillham
Aerial view of Cowplain tram depot – Mike Davies.
C.H.T. Marshall
Lillywhite Ltd
R. Elliott
G.N. Southernden
G.A. Tucker
S. Cribb
B.Y. Williams
Portsmouth News
T. Detheridge coll

Taken on an April day around 1930, here we see the junction of the Horndean Light Railway taking the tracks off the street tramway where Portsmouth to Cosham trams ran to Cosham railway gates terminus just out of site around the distant bend. It is at this point where the Portsdown & Horndean Light Railway began its journey to Horndean.

The street tramway is in Portsmouth Road and the Corporation tram tracks which terminated at Cosham railway gates. The light railway turned off at this junction opposite the Ports Bridge Hotel sometimes spelt Portsbridge Hotel.

The view has a slight optical allusion as you might think it took a sharp left off of Portsmouth Road but as will be seen it is really little more than a V junction with the track running alongside the Corporation tracks.

Having left the main Portsmouth Road from just outside the Ports Bridge Hotel the tram would run for a hundred yards or so before taking a bend to the right and passing over the railway line via an iron bridge. The route then headed through Cosham and northward over Portsdown Hilll to Horndean.

In May 1932 a reserve track was opened which ran straight from Ports Bridge through the junction of Northern Road and Portsmouth Road and the old lines to Cosham railway station became disused.

On the right a car No. 95 trundles by on route 8 on its way south through Portsea Island.

(Thanks to Martin Petch author *Portsmouth Tramways*, Middleton Press, for use of this photograph.)

The same scene today from outside the Ports Bridge Hotel and ninety-years difference. A park has now been established on the site of the former tramway with a sports ground a little further north. Unless there were photographs and postcards to show how it once was no one would have an idea a tramway once existed at this location.

With the coming of more comfortable and faster buses the Horndean Light Railway was abandoned on 9 January 1935.

In this view we are looking north with the Portsmouth Road to the right and Northern Road to the left. Emerging between the two roads we see a Corporation car leaving the reserved track opened in 1932. The unused tracks along the Portsmouth Road can be seen in the foreground. With a workman on the left this might be around the time the new track was opened to service.

In the distance on Portsdown Hill can be seen Fort Widley, one of the six forts built along the top of the hill to defend Portsmouth from attack from the north. What you see is the rear of the fort.

The same scene today with the very busy Northern Road lined with poplar trees. The tram would have emerged from the trees which now lighten the scene.

The road to the forefront is laid out for modern traffic in what is a very busy area during work commuting hours. Fort Widley is shrouded by greenery.

In this map we can see the original route through Cosham from where the P&HLR left the Portsmouth Road opposite the the Ports Bridge Hotel. Cosham compound is opposite Windsor Road.

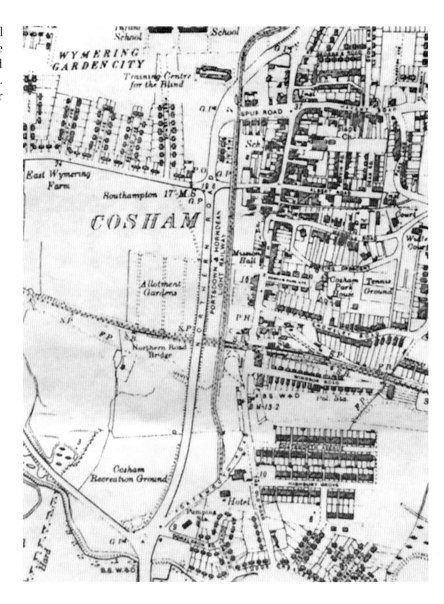

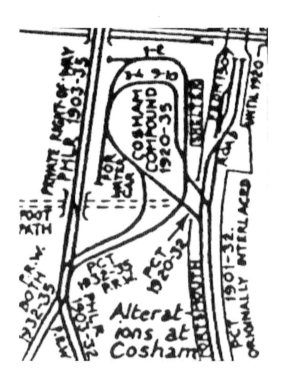

In this enlarged map of the area which is now a public park we can see the original track that led to Cosham railway station and the alterations at the level crossing.

To the bottom left we have the old P&HLR track 1903-1932 and the reserved track coming in from the lower left in 1932. Where the Horndean track runs there appears to be a bridge over a footpath but we have never seen a photograph to prove it. This is now a private road for buses to turn off of Northern Road and into a multi-bus stop area on part of the former Cosham compound. In recent years much of the former compound has had a block of flats built on it.

In this scene we are looking north with a Corporation car having left the reserved track and by a circular route it enters Cosham compound.

The P&HLR track led off to the left to head for interchange platform Point C from where a car can be seen leaving. It then passed over an iron railway bridge which crossed the Portsmouth to Fareham line. Fort Widley can again be seen on the ridge of Portsdown Hill.

Believe it or not, this is the same scene today with every trace of tramcar movement vanished from sight. This is now within a public park. The dog would be walking on the former reserved track.

While taking the image I was asked twice what I was taking photographs of. When I told my enquirers they had no idea whatsoever of what once ran beneath their feet.

O n a bright summer's day the tram conductor and
driver look towards to camera when heading for
Southsea. Northern Road can be seen on the left.

The same scene today with the tram and the employees long gone. The area is now part of the quiet Cosham Park although the Northern Road behind the weeping willow tree on the left is much busier than in tramway days.

Without a single passenger, a southbound car from Horndean arrives at Point C. To the forefront are the Corporation tracks leading to Cosham compound. Where the man is walking is where the private road for modern buses now turns down. Portsdown Hill looks somewhat bleak on this cloudy day.

A much smarter view than in the previous shot with lush trees and shrubs growing in place of the many poles that were needed to support the overhead wires. Where Point C was located there is now a tennis court. To the rear is Northern Road. Portsdown Hill is again hidden by foliage.

Here we see the remains of the track over the iron bridge over the railway line from Portsmouth to Fareham. The large building to the right is a cinema. The approach abutments from the south have already been removed.

This is a scene in the 1940s long after the trams had stopped running but the iron bridge over the railway remained in situ for many years after. The person in the car who survived this accident was a local doctor. As luck would have it I have a witness to the incident.

Eric Eddles told me: 'I joined the Portsmouth Building School in 1948 at the age of eleven. It was situated in Cosham Park House at the end of Cosham Park Avenue. Between Cosham High Street and the main A3 Northern Road lay a disused iron bridge which was once used by the Horndean Light Railway. This was a favourite place for my two chums and me to do our train spotting. One very memorable day on that red painted rusty bridge our attention was quickly drawn to our right as we heard a tremendous crashing noise. A goods train had reversed through the closed level crossing gates wrapping them around the signal box. There came a screeching metallic sound and we could see the cause of this terrific noise. A black Rover, typically used by doctors had at the exact time of the accident been on the railway lines between the gates. The car was now trapped upside-down beneath a wagon and was being pushed along by the reversing train. Just below us the wagon finally de-railed and everything came to a halt. How long we remained there I do not know. People rushed along the track to assist the driver – eventually miraculously getting him out and attempting to lay him on a stretcher. With profanities issuing from his mouth he stomped off towards the level crossing and that was the last we saw of him. The report of this accident appeared and stated that the driver in fact was – can you believe it – a doctor.'

Believe it or not but this is Cosham back in 1903. The tracks are all laid and ready to receive the first trams. Behind camera is where Waite Street roundabout and the police station are today. Either side of the newly laid tracks are fields and hedgerows and all very rural and countryfied.

To the right of the photograph is where the Northern Road was later built and opened in 1922. In the distance is the bridge over the railway line with Cosham station to the left but out of sight of course.

The tram tracks would have been a few yards to the left and run where the lift shaft on the right-hand side of the building can be seen today.

Looking north from the railway bridge and a reverse of the 1903 image. On Portsdown Hill is the ever present Fort Widley keeping guard over Portsea Island. Below it on the slopes is the Queen Alexandra Hospital. Everything is rural and countryfied.

The gap in the hedge shows where the track crossed the Southampton Road later called Waite Street. The ballast and track work are in excellent condition.

Here is the same vista today with the Northern Road running to the west of the old tram route. I had to stand some 20 feet to the right of where the tram lines actually ran otherwise all you would see is the wall of the now closed telephone exchange. The iron bridge over the railway remained in situ for many years after the end of service in 1935

If you are struggling with this photograph look up high on the hill – it is Fort Widley. Where the tram is going away from camera is where Cosham fire station is now located. The road crossing left to right the foreground is in fact what is now called Waite Street, but was then the A27 Southampton Road when it was the main road westward to Fareham.

The tramway had crossing gates to protect it but they appear to have been disconnected at this late date in the Portsdown & Horndean Light Railway's life. The tramway heading north would have then crossed Spur Road, Northern Road and then headed up the hill on the left side of London Road crossing Southwick Hill Road via a bridge.

This is the same scene at Waite Street crossing today. I stood up high so as to get a better perspective and to get Fort Widley in view as well. The modern fire station offices are built on the tram tracks.

The lady crossing the road is where the young couple were standing in the previous photograph. To the left out of camera the former Southampton Road is now Medina Road. Vast changes indeed since the P&HLR tram ran this route.

Seen crossing Spur Road, Cosham it appears as if the driver has stopped to let a passenger board the tram. At this time behind camera would have been a T-junction with the Northern Road. This remained so until the new Southampton Road was constructed in the 1940s. To the right can be seen Corporation buses parked up and behind them the old London Road heads south through Cosham.

Behind camera is the busy roundabout of Northern Road, Spur Road and Southampton Road. I ran into the road and took a quick photo while there was a gap in the traffic-about six seconds but I managed it with only one loud beep from an irate driver!

A triangular traffic island now sits where the tram driver allowed the passenger to board. The road into the distance is the old A27 leading to Havant and Chichester.

Pictured in the early 1930s we see a tram crossing the bridge over the Southwick Hill Road. The massive abutments hold back the embankment supporting the tramway. To the other side of the tramway bridge was a footbridge running parallel with it. Only a lonely cyclist makes his way up the A3 London Road towards the summit of Portsdown Hill.

As someone who takes hundreds of street photographs this is what I would call a nightmare scene. Traffic lights, street furniture, bollards and railings mar any photograph.

The bridge was removed in 1944 for scrap and the abutments removed in 1952 to widen the road (although not all that much). The footbridge remained in use for many years after but that has also since been removed. Trees and shrubs have since softened the scene

The tram trackbed where it crossed the Southwick Hill Road, Cosham circa 1903. A tram for Horndean approaches from the south on the up road.

As can be seen, the bridge is askew of the road beneath and runs on an embankment into the distance heading for Cosham.

The London Road, later the A3, can be seen below running into Cosham. There was no Spur Road or Northern Road back then. The Queen Alexandra Hospital, to the right out of camera, would have been for military use only.

This is the same view over Southwick Hill Road today with the former bridge demolished and the abutments overgrown.

At one time, and until recent years, there was a footbridge across the road at this point leading to the QA Hospital but, as can be seen, that has been demolished as well.

The formerly quiet London Road south to the Red Lion public house is now very busy. After 1922 Northern Road directed traffic from the London Road through Cosham to bypass it a hundred yards or so to the west. Housing now covers the land on the far side of London Road.

H ere we see Point A, the interchange point between Corporation cars and Light Railway cars. It was at this point the double track became single line.

As can be seen there are two former horse tramcar bodies to protect passengers from the wind and rain. This stop was located opposite Widley Lane and a flight of steps were laid to let passengers up from the pavement some 6 feet below track level.

Owing to the amount of trees and shrubs that have grown up over the last eighty years it is almost impossible to show where the locations are today from the top of Portsdown Hill. However, a later addition this location today at ground level. The concrete is nothing to do with the tramway.

Still in situ after being out of tramway use for 83-years. The steps up to the former Point A opposite Widley Road formerly Widley Lane. Walkers now use the steps as a leg up to a footpath where Point A was once located. Mind you, in autumn they are usually covered in overgrown blackberry bushes.

In this scene the children are sitting on the northern parapet of the underpass that once led to the fairground held two or three times a year on the west side of the London Road. The tram is still in the double track section so it must be approaching Point A.

To the rear can be seen the chalk pit excavations from the nineteenth century. A modern equivalent shot is difficult to achieve as everything is completely overgrown right down to the London Road on the right. All we would be looking at would be a massive shrubbery.

nother scene that is now completely obscured with hedges coming back as far as where the photographer stood. It is Point A once again with a railway-like semaphore signal protecting the single line. They were called clear-way signals and introduced in about 1923. Acting in the same way as a railway signal it showed a green light when the arm was down and a red light when the arm was at 90 degrees i.e. up.

In the signal seen, a car would clear the single line and then a 'skate' in the overhead trolley wire tripped the signal to red or on. This gave a warning to a car coming in the opposite direction to wait in a passing loop. As the first car cleared the single line a skate would reset the signal to green or off. The whole of this area is now one massive hedgerow.

The same scene today with everything overgrown and no sign of the London Road behind the high hedge.

The other side of the fence from the previous photograph shows a tram ahead of the semaphore signal. It seems that this location was a popular stopping off point as it was on a loop between Point A and the George Inn. Many strollers are out and about and a motorbike and sidecar take a peaceful ride down the quiet London Road.

Up the London Road today with the much overgrown hedgerow where the track once ran. This photograph was taken at 6am as it is such a busy road.

Quite recognisable even today. We are looking down the London Road from the top of Portsdown Hill. It is 1903 and the tram tracks for the line to Horndean have been laid but are not yet in service. Going downhill can be seen a horse-drawn bus followed by a loaded haywain.

To the right can be seen the tram rails laid at a higher level which were single line on a reserved track alongside the road. It then became a double-track street tramway passing the George pub on the summit of the hill. The former chalk quarry can be seen on the right. During World War Two tunnels were cut into these chalk faces for refuges from the blitz. Amazing to think this was the same rural road that Horatio Nelson would have travelled down a century earlier.

This is nearly the same view today. Unfortunately for me, in 1968 the embankment where the original photographer stood was bulldozed to make way for the new dual carriageway which runs to the east of the George in a cutting. Planners should really have thought things through don't you think?

The chalk quarries are now all overgrown since those long forgotten days. Under the grass verge where the single track joined the roadway I found some of the original track, still embedded in concrete. The original road ran to the far side of the photograph which is now a slip road to Portsdown Hill Road

Having come off the reserved single line onto the main London Road car No.3 heads for the George Inn at the summit of Portsdown Hill.

Meagre traffic climbs to the top. Chalk pits can be seen to the rear. In the distance is Horsea Island to the west of Portsea Island. Up until 1813 this climb was much steeper, higher even than the rooftop of the present day George Inn which was built much later.

Such a struggle did stagecoach horses have in dragging the stage up from Cosham that in the early part of the nineteenth century Napoleonic prisoners of war were set to work lowering the summit by some 50 feet.

The same scene in 2018. In 1967 the London Road past the George Inn with the crossroads across Portsdown Hill Road had become too dangerous and a new cutting was made behind the pub. This removed the high banking from where the previous photograph was taken.

The tram track joined the London Road where the distant lamppost can be seen above the white van. The old part of London Road is on the right. It is now a slip road onto the east/west Portsdown Hill Road along the summit. It runs from Bedhampton to Fareham.

Up and down cars on the summit of Portsdown Hill. The vista from this point was one of the best in the UK with a view over Portsea island across the Solent to Ryde on the Isle of Wight. To the west could be seen Southampton Water and on a good day the Needles lighthouse to the far west of the Isle of Wight. To the east could be seen the spire of Chichester Cathedral over 10 miles away.

As mentioned previously, the summit of Portsdown Hill was at one time as high as the rooftop of the house on the far right-hand side. No doubt the Belle-Vue Tea Gardens did a good summer trade. I wonder who Ken the boot maker was?

A look up to the George Inn today and something of a change.

The old London Road would have passed underneath where the two lamp post standards are today. The top of the trees on the left is where the old summit reached before the PoWs were set to work reducing the height. The Belle-Vue has long gone to be replaced by trees and shrubs.

Seen outside the George Inn on the summit of Portsdown Hill is a car full of people on a day out on the Portsdown & Horndean Light Railway. The conductor at the rear of the car is seeing passengers on board the car. I say 'summit' but as I explained earlier, the summit was some fifty feet higher than this location. Note the bicycles leaning against the wall.

The same location today. I am sure the tram cars would have loved to have travelled at 30 miles an hour. The George has been modernised of course with new windows and flowers along the window ledges. Much of the scene is hidden behind foliage.

Unfortunately, the magnificent vista looking over Portsea Island across the Solent to the Isle of Wight once to be had from the top of the car was lost when the new road bypassing the pub at a lower level to the rear opened in 1968.

The end – the last day of service on 9 January, 1935. Driver Fred Wells takes a stop on the crossroads outside the George Inn. In later years this would be a very busy location with London to Portsmouth traffic heading north and south and traffic from Bedhampton to Fareham crossing east to west. It all came to a halt in 1968 when, as mentioned previously, the George pub was bypassed in a cutting to the rear.

A modern bus emerges from the same location as the tram driven by Driver Wells. There is no crossroads at this point anymore. Traffic turns left to take a roundabout way to rejoin the old London Road. The George Inn is still trading as of 2019.

T his is a modern day photograph of the crossroads at the summit of Portsdown Hill. The old London Road crosses at the bottom of the gradient.

As mentioned earlier, up until 1813 this was a level road with a climb from Cosham arriving from the left. It must have been an horrendous pull for stagecoach horses. The George Inn is on the right and the modern London Road passes under the railings either side of the photograph.

The route from the George Inn was on a street tramway single-lined with passing loops, apart from through Waterlooville where it became double track once again. Relevant detail can be made out by the captions alongside. This map is accredited to J.C. Gillham in 1955.

Coming off the passing loop (or siding as it was called) at Purbrook Common with Purbrook Common Road 100 yards behind the tram. It is 8 September, 1934 and the cars have just a few months to run. Car 14 is on its way to Southsea with a through service. Notice the row of shops on the far right.

The same scene today with the shops all but hidden by shrubs. The road has been widened in recent years to add a bus lane. Purbrook Common Road on the left leads into the countryside and the shops on the right still trade.

Just a few yards north of the previous photograph and the track passes over a brook. A rural scene that was soon to change with modern traffic requirements.

Yes, the same scene today. Whereas Stakes Road used to join the London Road a quarter of a mile further on, today it has been diverted to join the road at this point. The brook still runs under the road and the bridge abutment is under the tree on the left. I had to stand further out in the modern road because of the overgrown shrubbery.

Something children could not do today: play in the London Road! We see a packed Car 13 heading north away from Purbrook village.

On the left is St John's church and the pub opposite is the Woodman. The shadows of the children make this an afternoon photo – about 3pm at a guess.

It appears quiet but I did take this photograph at 6am on a Saturday. At any other time there would have been a chance of being run over.

In November 1934 we see the Leopard pub in Purbrook, close to the pavement edge. The building this side of it is the generating station housing two 150BHP diesel engines. Mr Cobb the butcher would no doubt have a large delivery area, such was the sparse population in the village at the time.

All change at the Leopard. Not only was the original demolished and rebuilt further back from the pavement but its successor has also closed and is now a Co-op convenience store. Such is the way of the world these days. Cobb's butchery business has long since passed into history like the trams.

I am not so sure if this car is travelling in a northerly or southerly direction such is the angle of the pole. The car is approaching Mill Hill again through fields and a very rural area. Very few passengers are on board so it might be a winter's day. Butser Hill on the South Downs can be seen on the horizon through the mist.

More changes at Mill Hill with road widening and bus lanes in place. Behind the hedgerow on the left a vast housebuilding scheme is going on. Hundreds of houses are being erected increasing the population and the busyness of the road in future. The house on the right has the same chimney pots although central heating has no doubt taken over from an open fire.

Looking north along the London Road through Waterlooville circa 1925. There is very little traffic apart from one tramcar and a lorry. The Italianate building to the left is the Baptist church built in 1884 at a cost of £2000. It was demolished in the 1960s. North of the church on the other side of the crossroads is the Heroes of Waterloo Hotel built in 1890. A marvellous upper-floored mock-Tudor building it was demolished in 1966. A shopping centre was built on the rear of the site. A new pub simply called The Heroes was opened some 200 yards further north. The crossroads consisted of the London Road with Stakes Hill Road to the right and Hambledon Road to the left.

The London Road through Waterlooville today. Most of the old road is now a precinct. Before the A3M was constructed some mile or so to the east this was the main A3 London Road with continuous traffic all day and night. It all came to a stop when the new road was opened in the 1980s.

The Hambledon Road to the left of the former crossroads is now just 200 yards long as it meets the bypass to the west of the town and rejoins the old road at the MIlton Road roundabout.

A reverse of the previous historic photograph looking south and we see the Heroes of Waterloo on the right with the Baptist church on the other side of Hambledon Road.

Along the London Road through the village the track became double line until Hulbert Road was reached. It then passed onto a kerbside reserved track.

A modern view, with boring modern-constructed buildings holding sway. The former main London Road is now a precinct for its length to Hulbert Road, behind camera.

Londoon Road, Waterlooville at the junction with Hulbert Road on the right. It was at this spot the track passed on to a reserved track which it remained all the way to Horndean. Just a lone horse and cart travels on the main road to London.

The modern scene at the junction of Hulbert Road. This was another early morning photograph as the traffic is continuous throughout the day. To the left the roundabout takes traffic onto a bypass to the west of the town.

A very quiet London Road at the turn of the last century. The Edwardian figures seem to be out for the day and the car is carrying many passengers. What it must have been like to live in the pollution-free, car free era of yesterday. The former tram track would have been under what is now a modern bus lane the road being somewhat wider than in tramway days.

The same location but with modern traffic, although it is very quiet. All the modern street furniture that makes up today's roads are on show.

Looking north along London Road with the Spotted Cow pub on the left. Again. local people stroll about in the road whilst two cars can be seen on the right looking packed out with passengers.

A modern London Road. The Spotted Cow still serves local needs although a new building is set back from the road. Again the road has been widened to overlay the former tram tracks.

An aerial view of the Purbrook tram shed almost opposite Park Lane. Supplied by Mike Davies. He told me: 'The Tram Company finished in 1935 and the depot was closed. My grandfather, Jim Davies, was sent to Portsmouth from Cheshire by Fodens Limited to close their existing premises in Albert Road, Cosham and move the business to Cowplain following the purchase of the empty depot and Victoria House next door which became our family home. He then ran the business and was joined by his son, my father, Noel Davies and stayed until his retirement in 1952. My father then became manager and was eventually given the task of closing the business in 1966/67 when it was moved to Wandsworth in south-east London. The site was sold to Mr Ed Borrow of Padnell Grange Farm, Cowplain who had also acquired some adjacent property. The whole area was then sold and redeveloped, the key building being the Waitrose supermarket (now Lidl).'

From the picture it can be seen that a substantial extension to house heavy machinery was added to the rear of the building sometime between its original build in 1905 and 1935. The alterations to the front door openings were probably carried out by the Dockyard as the front section of the building was commandeered by Priddy's Hard during the Second World War and used as a torpedo store. Fodens were allowed to continue to use the rear access and that part of the building until it was handed back following the end of hostilities.

The tram shed at Cowplain in 1931. The three-road shed had internal doors half way along. The central road had a pit for underneath inspection. Just along from the entrance was a mile post stating Portsmouth 8 miles, Petersfield 9 miles.

To the left is the LIFU car, short for liquid fuel. It was an experimental car with liquid fuel used to heat the boiler.

Only two men were ever in charge of the LIFU car. Mr D. Bundy tended the engine which, once started, did not need any more attention. A Mr Chase was the conductor. The car was in use from 1896 until 1901. It was stored at North End depot until 1903 and after that date moved to Cowplain depot and initially used as an emergency vehicle for towing in broken down cars. Latterly it was used as an office. There is no record of its demise.

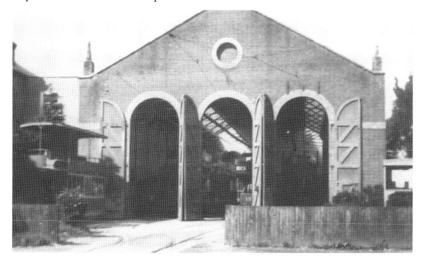

The shed was demolished in the 1960s and modern shops built on site. Here we see the same site today.

Cowplain tram shed almost completed. Here we see workmen digging out footings for the three-lane trackbed. The doors to the building have yet to have the arches fitted to the tops. Was it easier than fitting them when the doors were lying on the ground I wonder?

The three-way split tracks have been laid and await ballast and concrete. The workmen are wearing their own work clothes and not a bit of protective clothing in sight. I wonder if that is the foreman standing on the crossover?

The end of the line with the terminus just north of Horndean village in the distance. Two cars wait to depart. In 1919 the London Road was designated the A3. A former horsecar body acted as a waiting room in the early days. It was located just north of the Methodist chapel which still survives.

The same scene today. The A3M runs half a mile to the north the old road, crossing it by a bridge.

A final scene of the route and here we are looking south with the terminus just beyond the Methodist chapel marked with a cross. The dirt road must have been very dusty in high summer.

The same location today with several of the cottages now demolished. New housing to the right required an exit road and a traffic island, not needed in the slightest in tramway days, to give safe passage across the former A3.